To Rob and George, with love
K.W.

For Helen
M.B.

Other titles in the *Imagine* series:
Imagine you are a Tiger
Imagine you are a Crocodile

Text copyright © Karen Wallace 1998
Illustrations copyright © Mike Bostock 1998

First published in 1998 by Hodder Children's Books
This edition published in 2003 by Hodder Wayland

10 9 8 7 6 5 4 3 2

A catalogue record for this book is available from the British Library.

ISBN: 0 7502 43171

Printed and bound in Singapore by Imago

Hodder Children's Books
A division of Hodder Headline Limited
338 Euston Road, London NW1 3BH

Imagine you are a
DOLPHIN

Karen Wallace

Mike Bostock

HODDER
Wayland

An imprint of Hodder Children's Books

Imagine you are a dolphin,
Twirling, shiny in the water.
Others swim beside you,
Around you and underneath you.

A shiny dolphin sees his mother.
She swims beside her new baby.
If the baby wanders from her,
She drags his snout across the sand.

A shiny dolphin knows these lessons.
He's old enough to swim with others.
He's old enough to leave his mother.

Imagine you are a dolphin.

He roams the ocean like a seabird,

His skin is smooth like shiny satin.

He squeaks and whistles in the spray.

A dolphin dives into a canyon.
A shoal of fish flash past like shadows.
He herds them upwards like a sheep dog.
Other dolphins wait to catch them.

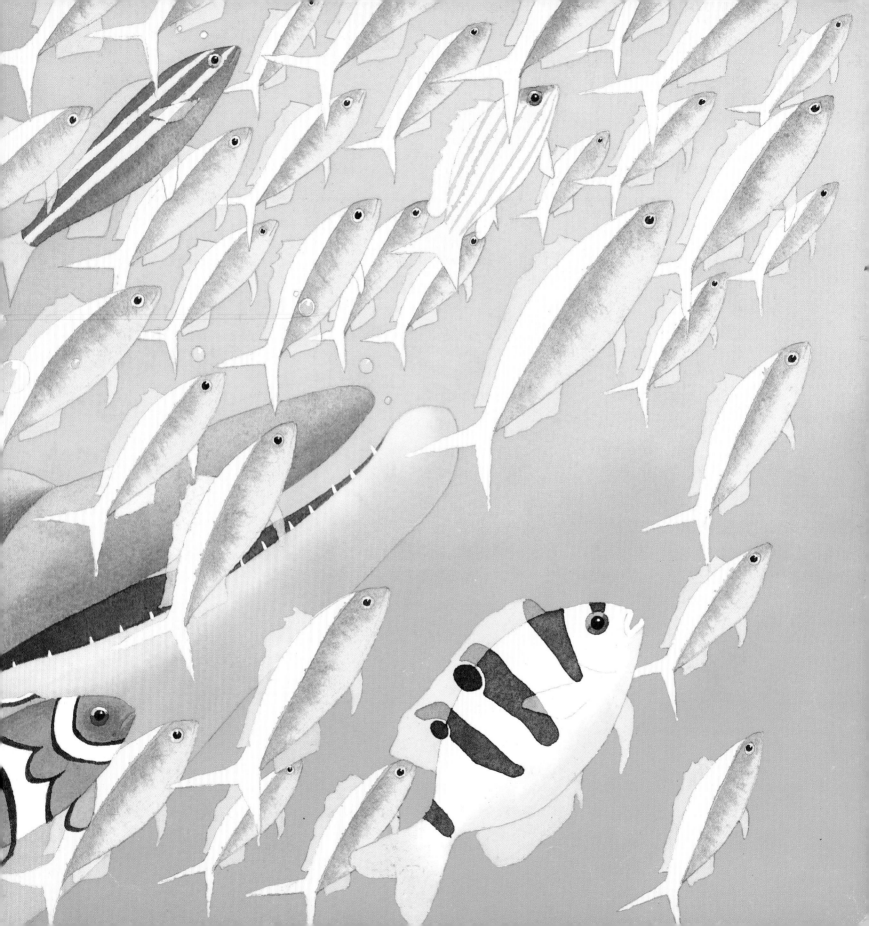

There are fish nets in the water.

The nets are death traps for a dolphin.

Some young dolphins leap inside them.

Other dolphins swim away.

Imagine you are a shiny dolphin, hesitating for a moment ...

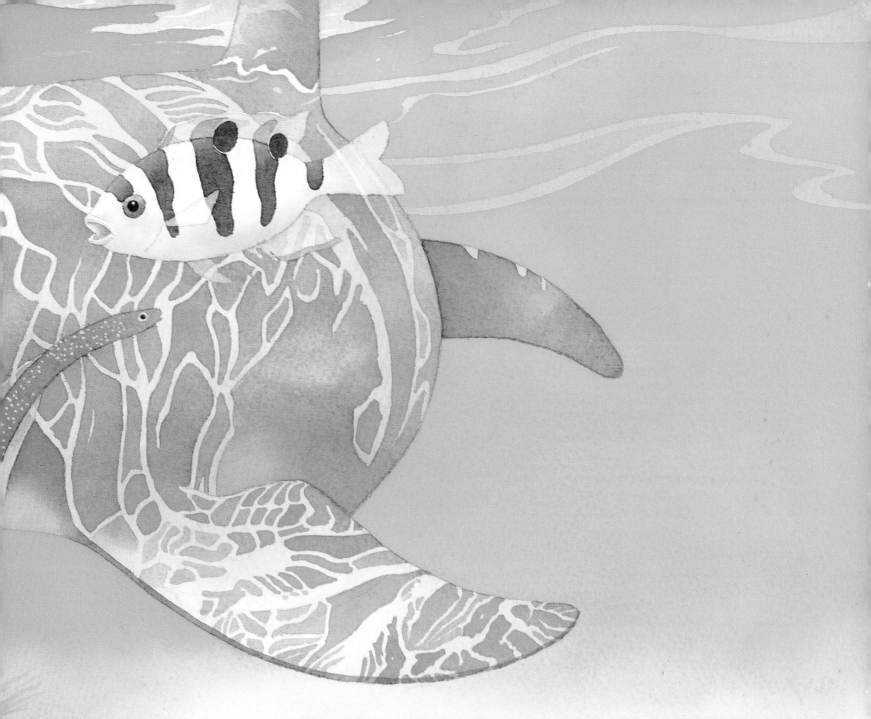

A shiny dolphin hunts for flat fish.

He burrows through the gritty seabed.

A sand eel squirms.

He gulps it down.

A shiny dolphin rides the storm waves.
He rides the bow waves of huge ships.
He turns with others like torpedoes.
They whizz like bullets
through the spray.

Imagine you are a speeding dolphin.
He rolls and zigzags through the water.
He does not hear the killer whales
Who sneak like submarines towards him.

A frightened dolphin leaps and squeals.
He races through the icy water.
A friend beside him swims too slowly.
The killer whales are quick and hungry.

A dolphin dives. The others follow.
He dives towards a pearly shadow.
He's found their feast deep in the ocean.
A shoal of squid glow in the darkness.

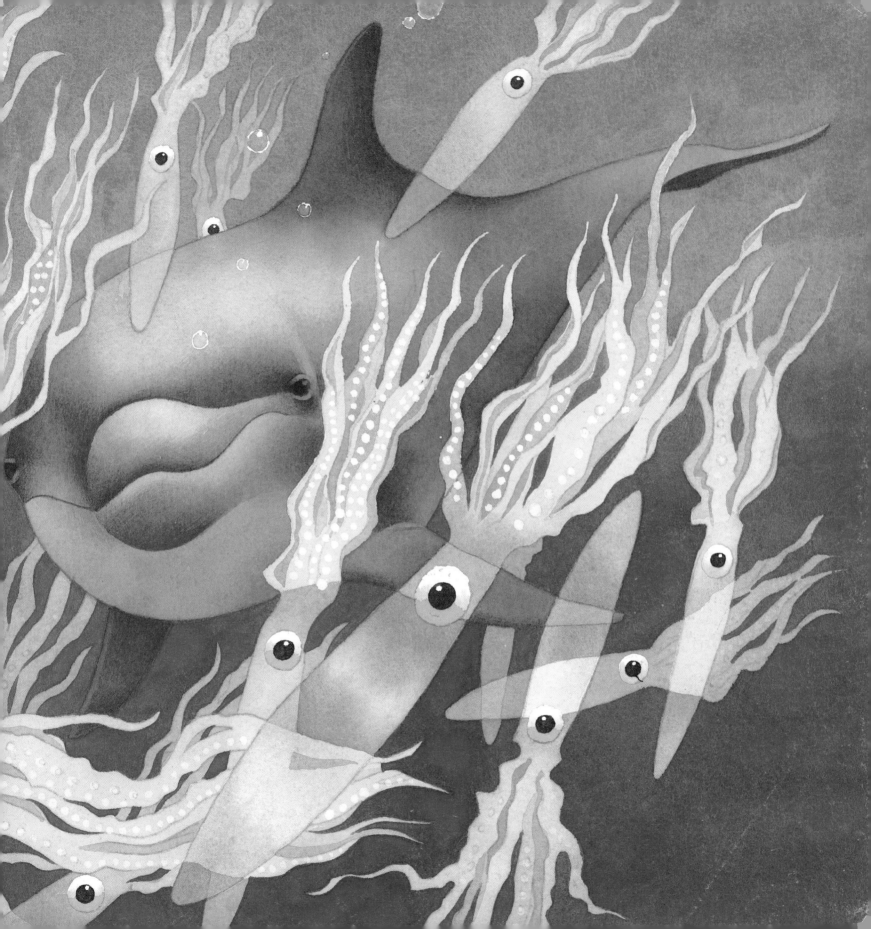

Imagine you are a shiny dolphin,
Full and joyful in the moonlight.
Other dolphins jump beside you.
They soar above the sparkling wave crests.
They play like children on the water.

Imagine you are a dolphin.